LAOCH (Lay-ock) The Guide Dog Puppy

Puppy Raiser: Lois Brussee

Written and Illustrated by Warren Brussee

Copyright © 2006 Warren Brussee

ISBN-13 978-1-60145-102-6
ISBN-10 1-60145-102-4

All rights reserved. No part of this publication may be reproduced, stored in a retrieval system, or transmitted in any form or by any means, electronic, mechanical, recording or otherwise, without the prior written permission of the author.

Printed in the United States of America.

Acknowledgements: Puppy-raising is only a small element of the training of a guide dog. Many other volunteers and professionals are part of this extensive process. The staff at Southeastern Guide Dogs, Inc. has been very supportive in the publication of this book; and Cheri Sims and Michelle McDonald gave valuable inputs. Special thanks are due Brigit Armbrister, who child-tested an early manuscript in her classroom. The detailed feedback from her enthusiastic students was invaluable for determining the tenor of the final book.

Booklocker.com, Inc.
2006

Hi! I am Laoch. I want to be a guide dog for the blind when I grow up.

When I was still a puppy, I was taken to my people mom and dad, who were called "puppy raisers." I was a little scared, but I could hardly wait to meet them. My new mom told me that she would love me and care for me until I got big, so I gave her a big lick!

My new mom and dad took me to their home, where I met Panda Bear, a Newfoundland dog. Panda was huge, but very gentle!

I was very tired after such an adventure. My mom had made me a cozy bed, so I settled down for a much needed night's sleep.

    The next morning I showed my new mom her puppy-raiser book. This book told her what to do in my training so I could grow up to be a guide dog.

I had to learn not to jump on people and to come when called. I also had to learn to walk on a leash without pulling. That was hard. I wanted to pull and go really fast.

    People weren't supposed to pet me when I was wearing my guide dog puppy-jacket, because I was "working!" Since I really liked people to pet me, this was hard.

    I had to sit before all doors and steps. Sometimes I would forget and Mom had to remind me.

Mom took me near big construction equipment and had the operators start their engines. I had to learn not to be afraid of the noise; but they were really, really loud!

As a guide dog puppy, I got to do things most dogs don't do. I even went on a small airplane. Mom brought along some towels in case I got sick!

When the plane took off, it was very noisy and I was afraid. Then Mom hugged me and I was okay.

I was flying. I was really flying! And I didn't get sick!

I got to ride on trains and buses. One bus was especially made for people in wheelchairs, and I had to ride up and down on the wheelchair lift. I liked doing that, and I wasn't afraid at all.

In libraries, it was hard not to eat the grape and cherry gum stuck under the tables. Mom told me I had to stop doing this.

I went to a state fair. There were lots of animals and rides, but what I really liked was the toss-the-ball-into-the-hoop game. I wanted to take one of the balls to play with, but Mom told me that I couldn't do that.

    When in restaurants, I had to stay under the table no matter how long it took my mom to eat. Sometimes I would stick my nose out just a little to watch all the people.

When I didn't have my guide dog puppy-jacket on, I liked playing tug-of-war with my friend Panda Bear. Panda was stronger than me and always won. But I was getting bigger and stronger every day!

Panda Bear and I liked to go swimming. Mom would throw floating toys into the water, and we would race to get them and bring them back to her.

Then she would throw them in again. And again! Mom would get tired of this before we would!

Sometimes I just hung out on our dock with my friend Liam. He liked to pretend to fish with his toy fishing rod. Sometimes he caught plastic fish!

   I liked walking through pumpkin fields with Reed. Reed would look at rocks while I sniffed the pumpkins.

In the evening, as the sun was going down, it was fun being out on the dock with Mom and Panda Bear.

Panda and I liked to lean against Mom. We both really liked her!

    I was now almost grown, and it was time to go back to school for my final training to become a guide dog. The evening before I had to leave, my two neighbor friends and Panda Bear said good-bye to me and wished me well. I was going to miss them.

    The next morning, my mom and dad drove me back to school. They told me they loved me, gave me big hugs, and told me to study hard. I gave them both big licks. It was really hard to see them leave!

Here is a picture that I sent my mom and dad from school. I am wearing my leather guide dog harness. I smiled as hard as I could for the picture!

I will soon meet my blind person and we will train together for a month. Then my mom and dad puppy raisers will come to my graduation and see me work as a real guide dog.

I will be really, really proud! I know they will be too!

Printed in the United States
76711LV00002B